LES
IMMORTELLES

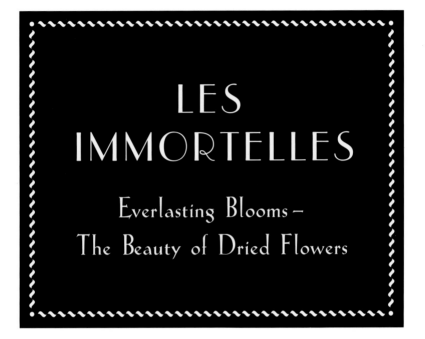

LES IMMORTELLES

Everlasting Blooms –
The Beauty of Dried Flowers

By Georgeanne Brennan and Kathryn Kleinman

❥•❥

Written by Georgeanne Brennan

Photography by Kathryn Kleinman

Flower Production by Michaele Thunen

Design by Jacqueline Jones Design

CHRONICLE BOOKS
SAN FRANCISCO

Library of Congress Cataloging-in-Publication Data:
Brennan, Georgeanne, 1943–
    Les immortelles: everlasting blooms—the beauty of dried flowers /
    written by Georgeanne Brennan; photography by Kathryn Kleinman;
    flower production by Michaele Thunen; design by Jacqueline Jones Design.
    p. cm.
    Includes bibliographic references (p.   ) and index.
    ISBN 0-8118-0672-3
    1. Everlasting flowers. 2. Everlasting flowers—Collection and preservation.
    I. Kleinman, Kathryn. II. Title.
SB447.B74 1995
635.9'736—dc20   95-1570
                                              CIP

Printed in Hong Kong.

Editing by Virginia Rich
Design assistance by Kristen Jester, Jacqueline Jones Design
Photography and production assistance by Terry Greene,
Cachet Bean and Helga Sigvaldadóttir

Distributed in Canada by
Raincoast Books
8680 Cambie St.
Vancouver, B.C.
V6P 6M9

10 9 8 7 6 5 4 3 2 1

Chronicle Books
275 Fifth Street
San Francisco, CA 94103

To Jim,
with love and thanks.
—Georgeanne

To my family and friends
and everyone who finds joy in
nature's unending beauty.
—Kathryn

Table of Contents

Introduction

Immortelle—everlasting, immortal, imperishable—all words associated with musings on the grand scheme of nature and life, words that suggest the endurance of granite, the permanence of finely carved marble, the timelessness of love, loyalty, and devotion. It seems not inappropriate that *immortelle* also refers to flowers, those tokens of remembrance that appear at the intense moments of our lives, whether celebratory or mournful. Flowers in all their forms—fresh, dried, rendered in porcelain or wax, in paintings or in beadwork—adorn equally the bassinet, the bridal bower, and the bier.

Dried flowers, *les immortelles*, have a notable place in the pantheon of flowers because they endure, retaining the essence of the fresh flower yet having a unique identity. It is this duality that fascinates. Dried flowers are not simply substitutes for fresh flowers but another manifestation of them, whether turned into fantastical designs by artists, made into traditional wreaths and garlands, or simply left to dry in their natural shape. The idea of imperishable, immortal flowers has abided through the centuries and continues to intrigue us today.

In general horticultural terms, *les immortelles* are flowers whose papery petals keep their color and form even after being picked. Because of this, they are called everlastings, and the group includes such common flowers as sea lavender, statice, strawflower, Cupid's dart, and pearly everlasting. In a narrower and more restrictive sense, *les immortelles* refers to only one of the everlasings, *Helichrysum bracteatum*, or strawflower. However, in the last seventy to eighty years, the term *everlastings* has broadened to include not only flowers with papery petals but any flower that is commonly dried, such as yarrow, Queen Anne's lace, and love-in-a-mist. Gathered from the wild, garden grown, hothouse or field grown, sand-dried, air-dried, pressed, waxed, or freeze-dried, *les immortelles* today comprise the entire spectrum of the plant world, from vines to fruits and vegetables to flowers of every form. It is in the broadest sense that our book invites you to view *les immortelles*.

GROWING
AND
GATHERING

In the past, as today, certain flowers and plants were cultivated specifically with the intent of drying them for use in ornamentation. They were grown in both the great estate gardens of the nineteenth and early twentieth centuries and in the small pleasure gardens of the middle-class homeowners of the same period. Other flowers were planted primarily for cut flowers but were then dried as well, either by design or by chance.

During the Victorian period in England, any sizable estate or manor house had extensive gardens and a garden staff to oversee every aspect of the grounds, hothouses, orchards, and kitchen garden. It was in the kitchen garden alongside the rows of beans, beets, chard, and other vegetables that the flowers for cutting were planted. The everlasting flowers—those grown to be dried—were planted in the cutting garden as well. An estate's demand for cut flowers to supply both the town house and the country house was so enormous that William Robinson, a notable

English garden journalist of the late nineteenth century, remarked that the cutting gardens, like the estate's kitchen gardens, needed to be managed like a production market garden. Production gardens, unlike pleasure gardens, must before all else produce a certain volume on a regular schedule throughout the growing season. Because the growing season for fresh cut flowers ended with the frosts of winter, it was the everlasting flowers that were used to compose *bouquets d'hiver* — the arrangements of dried flowers that ornamented the house in winter.

In spring when seeds and seedlings were planted for summer's and fall's cut flowers, seeds of *les immortelles* were planted to produce enough dried flowers for winter, when only hothouse flowers would otherwise be available. Helichrysum in shades of carmine, violet, and cream, blue-and-silver Cupid's dart, and sea lavender were among the everlastings that were commonly planted in the kitchen garden, providing orderly and attractive borders of summer color until harvested and taken to the drying rooms. Among the flowers that were picked from the garden grounds and dried

Seedsmen of the Nineteenth Century

Dozens of varieties of *les immortelles were offered by seedsmen of the nineteenth century, a testimony to the importance of
these flowers. For example, in 1883 the French seed company Vilmorin-Andrieux listed eighteen different colors and types of helichrysum,
two of acroclinium, five of globe amaranth, and three of pearly everlasting and fifteen different varieties of sea lavender.
The seeds, as well as plants, were sold in their shop on the Quai de la Mégisserie along the river Seine where it had been established
since 1745. Similar seed shops existed in London and the other major cities of Europe, but as times changed and the cities
spread out and overran the surrounding rural areas, the seed shops closed or moved, following their agricultural clients.
The Vilmorin-Andrieux shop stayed in place. It is still there today, called simply Vilmorin.*

were roses, hydrangeas, and the newly popular pansies. Unlike the flowers from the production garden, however, the random collection of pansies and roses to be dried was likely the handiwork of one of the members of the household rather than of the garden staff.

Those of the middle class who were able to afford the luxury of owning land that did not need to be economically productive had landscaped grounds, pleasure gardens, and kitchen and cutting flower gardens as the upper classes did, albeit on a smaller scale. Informed and fascinated by the popular press, which was writing about global explorers who brought exotic plants back to the Royal Botanic Gardens at Kew and elsewhere, people of the middle class were also enthusiastic supporters of the floral exhibitions and competitions that flourished during the nineteenth and early twentieth centuries. The middle classes, too, grew *les immortelles* and dried them for *bouquets d'hiver*, fancied the latest roses, and tried their hand at hybridizing to create new roses themselves. They filled garden spaces with the latest in bedding plants, ornamental shrubs, and whatever exotica

they could grow. The upper classes, of course, on their grand estates employing dozens on the gardening staff, were able to have not only elaborate gardens but also the supporting infrastructure of hothouses, cold frames, conservatories, and glasshouses.

Few of us today have estates or gardening minions, but many of us have gardens or a bit of ground where we would like to have a garden, or even a window box. We can purchase the same seeds that the estate gardeners and amateur gardeners of the nineteenth century purchased to grow the various papery-petaled *immortelles* for *bouquets d'hiver*. Numerous varieties of larkspur, rudbeckia, and China asters are available to us, some that the Victorians grew plus many that have been introduced since their time. Although few of the seed strains for the pansy and violet varieties that were available a hundred years ago are still commercially available, there have been numerous new varieties of pansies developed, giving us a great array from which to choose.

Like pansies and violets, larkspur, roses, rudbeckia, and asters, many other flowers that are favorites from the cutting garden, flower beds, and flowering landscape shrubs are as enticing dried as they are fresh. Lush peonies, multipetaled or singlepetaled, make exceptional dried flowers, and their shape is readily maintained when they are dried in sand or silica gel. Hydrangeas, of which there are dozens of species in colors from creamy white to watercolor shades of green and violet and in shapes from lacy, dangling clusters to tightly formed snowball heads, were very popular in nineteenth-century gardens and are highly regarded today, both fresh and dried. Tulips, daffodils, and narcissus, which are rarely thought of as dried flowers, make excellent subjects, especially the less common species tulips, whose tiny size and unusual shapes surprise and delight.

Cultivated gardens were not the only sources for *les immortelles* in the nineteenth century. It was considered *de rigueur* to bring back flowers, leaves, seed pods, or bits of moss or lichen as souvenirs of travels abroad and excursions into nature. During the Victorian era, travelers pressed and put into albums such flowers as blue gentian picked during a summer walk in an alpine meadow or a fragrant sprig of flowering rosemary gathered from a stroll along the hillsides above the Mediterranean Sea. Once home, the albums, often annotated, were displayed and, like photographs, provoked drawing room reminiscence and conversations about the scenery, events, and people that comprised the whole of the experience. Dried berries, nuts, and seedpods, along with seashells or pebbles that might have been gathered during one's travels, were arranged into collections and showcased on tabletops or inside specially constructed glass-topped, glass-sided tables.

Sometimes the flowers or pods preserved were not from a trip but from a special occasion. Violets, rosebuds, orchids, and multihued autumn leaves were commonly tucked between the pages of a book, where they were kept as mementos of a dance, a dinner, or a night at the theater.

In a more disciplined fashion than the pleasure traveler, but with equal intensity and enthusiasm, amateur and professional

botanists of the nineteenth century collected and recorded plant life for scientific purposes. Men and women roamed the globe collecting flowers, grasses, and plant specimens of all kinds. Pressed, and then carefully mounted and labeled on folio pages, their findings became important records of the plant kingdom. These old herbaria seem to me like works of art. The angular or curving forms of the plants long-since dried, their once brilliant colors now turned to sepia, beige, muted rose, and rust colors, have the added quality of being a physical link to another time and place.

But pausing on a trail or a roadside to pick up a seedpod or an early spring flower that catches one's fancy is not an exercise that ended with the Victorian age, nor is the amateur collecting of plant specimens. Many of us recall making our own early pressed plant collections—mine I remember quite clearly. It was made with a bright green posterboard cover and black scrapbook pages and laced together with black yarn. Inside were carefully pressed samples of grasses and flowers that grew in the vacant lots in my neighborhood, as well as

PAINTED GARDENS

⁓ ⁓

At their shop in Paris, the French seed company of Vilmorin-Andrieux offered alluring representations of their flower and
vegetable seeds with original watercolors displayed in oversize leather-bound folios. The paintings were done by several different artists
who were brought to the company's growing grounds in Verrieres, southwest of Paris. Here, between 1877 and 1893, the artists
painted examples of the more than a thousand varieties of seeds, bulbs, and tubers that the company propagated and sold. Unlike botanical
illustrations, these watercolors had the purpose of selling the seeds. Consequently, the paintings were embellished with icons
of daily life. Helichrysum, acroclinium, and yarrow were illustrated dried, in an extravagant bouquet d'hiver; alpine ranunculus
and forget-me-nots were depicted clinging to the edge of a wild-looking cliff; plump, pointed-root white turnips were shown in a bundle,
wrapped with twine ready to sell at the market. Canary creeper, a popular houseplant of the era, was illustrated growing
with its long curling vines cascading from an urn centered on an ornamental table.

a few that I collected from the nearby hills or from the edges of the beach a few blocks away. In my very best ninth-grade handwriting I wrote out both common and Latin names on little white labels and I glued them next to the pressed plant.

My walks and rambles continue to yield gathered flowers and grasses, if not for pressing, then for bouquets. The first wild oats still tinged with green, a lacy stem of Queen Anne's lace, or long-stemmed pods left behind by wild poppies are all good candidates for gathering, as are bark and mosses.

It is almost impossible for me to be in a forest without bringing home a piece of moss. As a child, I listened as my mother regaled me with fairy tales and fantasies in which what the fairies were wearing and how their homes were furnished were as important to the story as the adventures and misadventures of the characters. Sleeping fairies and elves lay tucked beneath fluffy moss blankets dotted with tiny blossoms of wood hyacinth. The castle floors of knighted muskrats and the warrens of dashing rabbit-princes were made snug with carpets of tufted emerald green moss, smooth to the touch like velvet, and the cottage windows of homely little field mice were hung with gossamer Spanish moss, neatly tied back with twists of wild grapevine.

Gathered from forest, meadow, or roadside, cut from gardens large or small, grand and imposing or simple, flowers destined to become *les immortelles* have as much a place in our lives today as they did in the lives of people who have gone before us. Our vision of beauty may differ, but the appeal of imperishability and permanence remains.

AIR-DRYING

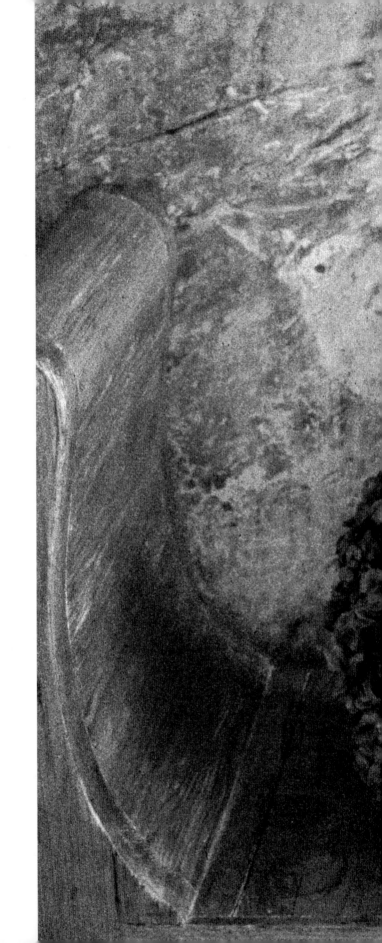

The simplest method for drying cut flowers, grasses, or other plants is to place them in a warm, dry environment with adequate air circulation and allow their moisture to evaporate. Air temperatures for drying can range from 50 to 120 degrees Fahrenheit, but there should be air circulation sufficient to remove moisture fast enough to prevent molds setting in before drying is complete. For maximum color retention, the drying locations should be dark: exposure to light causes the pigments in the plants to break down. If muted earth tones such as buff and brown are desired, there is no need to shut out the light.

There are three main air-drying techniques—hang-drying, flat-drying, and upright-drying. The choice of technique depends upon the growth habit of the plant and upon the effect desired. Hang-drying renders straight stems and precisely positioned flower heads and may be used for most kinds of flowers and grasses.

Flat-drying on racks is particularly suitable for thick, fleshy sunflower heads and for heads of heavily petaled, dense flowers such as cactus dahlias and beehive

zinnias, and also for stemmed flowers whose asymmetry and curves are sought, such as sweet-pea vines and old-fashioned clustered roses.

Flat-drying on trays or between sheets of folded newspaper is adequate for drying large light petals such as those of tulips, roses, and peonies as well as whole flower heads of the papery-petaled narcissus and daffodil. Branches, grasses, and foliage that are already rather dry may be placed between sheets of newspaper and laid flat in layers to finish the drying process.

Some grasses, such as headed wheat and rice and other nearly dry plants like curly dock and cattails, may be dried by placing them upright in containers with no further treatment. Upright drying in evaporating water is a technique that is particularly useful for achieving a natural, curving or nodding appearance. Placing stemmed flowers upright in containers with a few inches of water allows the flowers to dry slowly and naturally, yet without wilting as the water evaporates, a technique that is ideal for drying rose bouquets, single-petaled zinnias, and hydrangeas.

HARVESTING FOR AIR-DRYING

Flowers

For flowers or other plants that are to be
air-dried, the moment of harvest is important. If harvested too early, they may be
limp and look wan when dried, yet if
harvested too late they may drop their
petals or leaves after drying, leaving only
stems or seed heads. Although there is
some leeway, each type of flower has its
optimum moment, and that is of critical
importance in commercial dried-flower
production. Most commercially dried flowers and plants will be boxed, shipped, and
stored, then perhaps shipped again, before
finally being composed into arrangements
or adapted for other uses; harvesting at the
optimum moment maximizes sturdiness
and lessens the risk of an inferior product.
As a rule of thumb, most types of flowers to
be air-dried should be harvested when the
blooms are one-half to three-quarters open.
There are, of course, exceptions, such as
acroclinium—one of the most important
of *les immortelles* in the nineteenth century
and still of significance today—which must
be harvested only after the flowers are
fully opened and their round, bright yellow
centers fully visible.

Grasses

Grasses may be harvested green, before
seed heads have formed, or later when the
seed heads have formed and the grasses
are turning gold.

Garden Seedpods

Whole seedpods gathered from the garden,
such as tulip, iris, wisteria, poppy, radish,
and okra, may be harvested while the pods
are still green yet firm to the touch, or they
may be left longer in the garden to harden
and turn to beige-green. Burst pods, their
seeds dropped and scattered, may be harvested at any time.

Wild Things

Responsible foragers never strip a site of
a species of flowers, grasses, or shrubs and
do not gather from any property without
authorization from the owner. They
attempt to disturb as little as possible the
natural cycle of a particular environment
and generally gather seedpods from the
wild only after those pods have burst and
dropped their seeds.

Hang-Drying Lavender

Harvest: When the flowers are in the bud stage. Opened flowers will drop once dried.

Bundle size: Thirty to fifty stems. Space bundles approximately six inches apart to allow for adequate air circulation.

Hang-drying flowers, generally in bunches, is the most commonly used air-drying technique, suitable for almost any flower, grass, or herb. The plants should be freshly gathered and free of excess moisture. Strip the leaves from flower stems if you think that the leaves will interfere with air circulation and allow mold to develop after bunching. If you particularly want to keep the leaves, hang the stems singly. The number of stems per bunch will depend upon the type of flower, grass, or herb, with small-flowered varieties generally in more numerous bunches than large-flowered. Gather your stems into bunches no larger than a loose handful. Once gathered, bind the stems together with an elastic band or tightly wrapped string or cord. As the stems dry they will shrink, and if they are not well bound, they will slip apart. The completed bunches can now be hung in a warm, dark, dry place such as a large closet or attic where they will be safe from direct sunlight and nibbling insects.

The amount of time needed to complete drying depends upon the type of flower or grass and the temperature and humidity. It may take only a few days for a five-stem bunch of roses to dry, but two weeks for a three-stem bunch of alliums. Once dried, the hanging bunches may be left in place until you are ready to use them, or they can be removed, carefully wrapped in paper, and put in cardboard boxes. The boxes should be stored in a dry, moisture-free environment.

Lavender, with its haunting intense fragrance, is commonly hang-dried. Although we have come to think of cultivated lavender fields as synonymous with Provence, the flowers were originally gathered wild from the hillsides and was not a cultivated crop there until after World War I. Now in Provence *touffes* of gray-green foliage and spikes of glowing purple flowers cover several thousand acres in undulating rows acros plateaus and down the flanks of steep hillsides. Of the various varieties of cultivated lavender, the one most frequently grown in France for commercial production is the hybrid lavandin, the result of spontaneous hybridization in the wild of two different lavenders, *Lavandula angustifolia* (also called *L. vera* and *L. officinalis*) and *Lavandula latifolia*.

At the turn of the century when gatherers were cutting the wild lavender, they noticed some plants that were considerably larger than others, with longer flower stems and more flowers. In 1927 it was ascertained by laboratory analysis that this *grosse*, or big, lavender was indeed a hybrid. These larger, more productive plants were more desirable than either *L. angustifolia* or *L. latifolia*, and by 1975 almost all the commercial plantings in France were of one of three main selections of lavandin. Because hybrids do not grow true from seed, lavandin is propagated vegetatively, by a process that induces cuttings from a parent plant to sprout roots and branches.

However, *L. angustifolia*, which I grow at home in California, makes wonderful dried flowers, full of resinous fragrance that lasts and lasts. Some of our lavender is sold to the wholesale fresh flower market, but most of it is purchased by buyers who hang it themselves to dry. I like to cut the

HAUTE PROVENCE, LAVENDER HARVEST

Today, the vast fields of lavender are harvested by machine and the cut flowers loaded into large trucks that travel back and forth from the fields to the distilleries. But some lavender is still cut by hand for the fresh and dried flower market as it was a hundred years ago. At the end of the nineteenth century and into the twentieth, families and extended families left their villages or farms and each summer went to the mountains to cut lavender. Arriving at dawn, they started cutting the wild lavender with hand sickles. A big cloth, called an apron, was laid out and the cut lavender piled into it until the four corners of the cloth could just barely be brought up over the lavender to be tied in a knot. The lavender was priced and sold by the "apron-bundle." The harvest lasted a week or more, and those who were the main cutters slept out in a stone shepherd's hut or barn, while others ferried the lavender bundles down from the hills to the distillery and brought food and other supplies back up.

stems with some of the also-fragrant foliage attached and make them into thick haystacks of bundles, tied with raffia or heavy cord. To do this successfully the bunches must be tied loosely enough to allow ample air circulation for drying, otherwise, the leaf and stem mass will heat up and mold will grow. In all but the driest conditions, the leaves should be stripped from the stems before bunching and hanging.

Roses, suited both to upright-drying in evaporating water and to hang-drying, are perhaps the most universally appealing of all flowers, fresh or dried. There are well over twenty thousand named varieties in existence with great variation in the shapes, growth habits, and colors of the flowers and plants, so one could spend years experimenting with drying different varieties. The high, pointed buds of today's popular modern hybrid tea and floribunda roses unscroll into elegant, high-pointed blooms that produce a dried rose completely different in appearance from the old garden roses that once reigned supreme over the rose world.

Drying Roses Upright
in Evaporating Water

Harvest the roses as for hang-drying. Fill a container or vase one-quarter full of water. Place single stems of roses in the water, three or four per container. Put the container in a warm, dry, dark place.

Old garden roses, currently enjoying a renaissance among floral stylists and gardeners alike, are frequently characterized by rather flat or rounded buds that open to variations of flat-topped cups of densely packed petals organized in quadrants around a tight button center. 'Souvenir de la Malmaison', an old Bourbon rose that bears large, heavily fragrant blooms of blushed ivory cream, and 'William Lobb', an equally fragrant moss rose whose midsize blooms are deepest magenta, are good examples of the old rose shape, as are the cabbage roses (*Rosa centifolia*), which were so often depicted in Flemish paintings of the seventeenth and eighteenth centuries. The old garden roses, with the exception of the tea roses, have a color range limited to shades of pink, magenta, purple, and white. The teas have light yellow and buff as well as pinks.

The now-familiar rose colors of bright yellow, orange, apricot, and all their hues and shades did not appear in garden roses until after the development of the hybrid tea rose. A French rose breeder, Joseph Pernet-Ducher, succeeded in introducing

Hang-Drying Roses

Harvest: When the flowers are in bud with two or three petals beginning to unfurl, or when blooms are one-half to three-quarters open. If full-blown roses are used, the petals will fall.

Bundle size: Five to six stems for most single-stem blooms; two to three stems for floribunda roses and others with multiple blooms per stem.

the bright yellow color of the wild species rose *Rosa foetida* 'Persiana' into the hybrid tea roses in the late 1880s. Some of the early hybrid teas from the late nineteenth and early twentieth centuries have unusual and subtle colors and shadings that reflect their close proximity to the tea roses and the early introduction of yellow. It is rewarding to experiment with drying these if you are growing them or can locate some, because they are distinctly different from the hybrid teas of the later period.

Floribunda roses, developed in the early part of the century, provide an entire bouquet of roses on a single stem, unlike the hybrid tea, which ideally produces a single bloom per stem. Although for the most part floribunda buds are like those of hybrid teas, there is a great deal of variation among the flower shapes and colors. Some of the colors are to be found nowhere else in rose-dom. Delicate mauves tinged with lavender-brown, coffee cream fading to pink, amber yellow with a brownish cast, russet browns, tan touched with pink and yellow are all to be found among the floribundas. 'Lavender Pinocchio', 'Julia's Rose', 'Brownie', and 'Café' are some to look for, as unusual dried as they are fresh.

It is in the English roses introduced over the past thirty years by the breeder David Austin that one finds roses that exhibit the fragrance and the bud and flower shapes of the old garden roses but in a color range as wide as that of the modern roses. Deep crimson, magenta, blush pink, buff yellow, glowing apricot, fragile pinks, and shades of salmon and white are found in the large, flat, double and semidouble cupped flowers that bloom throughout the season.

Each year, hundreds more new roses are introduced by breeders, while dedicated old-rose nurseries are propagating and commercializing an increasing number of once-forgotten varieties. The dried results vary from rose to rose, of course, but there are so many different varieties from which to choose and air-drying is so easy that you need not hold your curiosity in check. Do note, however, that most roses dry to a darker color than that of their fresh form.

I like to dry entire bouquets containing fifteen to twenty stems of roses of different kinds, especially the mauve, pale lavender, tan, and coffee cream colored ones, along with those in shades of ivory and faint blush pink. I remove all the leaves, cut the stems to an even length, and bundle them together one-third down the stem length with ribbon before putting them in a container in a dry, dark place. Alternatively, I fill a vase one-half full with water and put it in a window that receives direct sun. As the water evaporates and the bouquet dries, the roses fade to shades of peach, buff, sienna, and dusty violet.

AIR-DRYING OUTDOORS

Flowers and plants may be left growing in the garden to dry naturally as they enter senescence near the end of their season. This method of air-drying is successful only in warm, dry climates, but spectacular results can be achieved. Consider a towering hollyhock, dried to a creamy tan, entwined with morning glory vines and their seedpods, or equally tall stalks of corn wound with the vines and pods of the climbing beans they supported.

Plants may also be cut or even uprooted and then hung or spread outside to dry. If kept in a sheltered environment they may retain much of their color. Chiles, grapes, and figs are dried this way, as well as beans and protea.

Be forewarned, though, that plants left to dry outside, whether still in the garden or cut and hung, are more likely to fall prey to pests than those kept inside.

Flat-drying on racks is a useful method for large, fleshy, thickly petaled flower heads and heavy-skinned vegetable, flower, and fruit pods. Racks may be constructed of wood, plastic, or metal and covered with screens or mesh. Regardless of the material used, the principle is to maximize exposure to the warm, dry circulating air in order to remove moisture from the plants before mold or decay can begin.

Flower heads may be trimmed to a short stem length, the stem may be removed entirely, or an artificial stem may be made from a piece of wire. Flowers with stems are inserted through the holes in the screen or mesh, flower head facing upward. Stemless flowers are placed on the rack face up, and fruits such as oranges and pomegranates and large pods like those of wisteria are simply placed on the racks and turned occasionally.

Table arrangements are easily created with
air-dried objects from nature. A walk through
the garden or woods reveals a multitude of
treasures for gathering and collecting. Even a
simple scattering of air-dried flowers adds a
whimsical and pleasing surprise to a party table.

Sunflowers of all types may be air-dried, but sunflower varieties that have fully developed fleshy heads, such as the classic large-disk types, are best dried upright on racks allowing for maximum air circulation. The smaller-disk sunflowers, particularly the side stems of the branching sunflowers, such as the multihued 'Autumn Beauty' and 'Evening Sun', or golden yellow types, dry quite well using the hang-drying method.

Unlike many flowers, whose primary purpose is decorative, the sunflower's most important use worldwide is as a source of vegetable oil, and secondarily it is food both for people and for birds and animals. Because of their economic importance, sunflowers have been the subject of plant breeding for many years. When a hybrid is created, the seed of the hybrid will not breed true, but will revert to one or more of the parents in its lineage. Many of the classic sunflowers that now appear in florist's shops and green market flower stalls are hybrids developed by the Japanese seed industry for the floral trade, and most

lately are male-sterile so that they do not produce and shed pollen, a desirable trait for cut flowers. Most of the hybrids are *Helianthus annuus* with yellow or gold multiple-ray petals surrounding a center disk of brown or golden green. The disk is large compared with the ray petals, resembling the proportions of the common giant

Hang-Drying Sunflowers

This method is particularly successful for sunflowers that have neither heavy, fleshy heads nor thick, fibrous stems.

Harvest: When the ray petals are three-quarters open and before any seed development is apparent. Leave ten to twelve inches of stem, plus a few leaves.

Bundle size: Three to five stems. Space bundles six to eight inches apart.

Drying time: Approximately two to three weeks.

sunflower. The flowers bloom on single stalks of uniform height, generally four to five feet, and are suited for winter hothouse production as well as for field production during the temperate months.

Sunflowers in shades of rusty brown, dark red, golden brown, reddish pink, and bronze are for the most part not hybrids but the result of breeding selections of open-pollinated types, primarily branching sunflowers, either *Helianthus annuus* or *H. debilis*. These may grow as tall as eight feet, with the first bloom at the top of the central stalk and side shoots with smaller flowers on short to medium-long stems. Generally the disk size is considerably smaller relative to the band of ray petals and seems more akin to that of a black-eyed Susan than a sunflower.

Oranges, lemons, limes, and pomegranates are thick-skinned fruits that are simple to air-dry on racks. As the moisture from the skin evaporates, the skin shrinks and becomes hard, forming a sealed cover

Rack Drying Lemons, Limes, Oranges, and Pomegranates

Harvest: Lemons, limes, and oranges should be harvested when fully ripe and yellow with at least one-quarter inch of the stem intact. If the skin is broken, the fruit may not dry successfully. Pomegranates may be harvested when slightly underripe or fully ripe and with no cracks or breaks in the skin.

Spacing: Place fruits four to five inches apart on the racks and turn occasionally.

Drying time: Approximately two weeks.

over the pulp and seeds inside. Once the skin has hardened, the fruits may be considered dry, even though the pulp and seeds inside may take many more months to dry completely.

Limes in particular dry very quickly, but their bright green exterior often turns to a brownish olive color as it shrinks and drys. 'Meyer' lemons and 'Moro' blood oranges both have rather small amounts of pith, the white spongelike layer just beneath the skin, and so dry more successfully than thicker-pithed varieties of oranges and lemons. Both lemons and oranges darken as they dry, the lemon becoming mustard-colored and the blood orange turning a deep copper color tinged with vermilion. Pomegranates dry quite well, darkening only slightly.

PRESSING

The principle of pressing flowers or plants to dry them is simple. Placed between sheets of absorbent paper, subjected to pressure, and kept in a warm, dry location, the plant is flattened and its moisture absorbed by the paper. The faster the drying, the more likely color and form will be retained. No doubt we have all slipped a flower between the pages of a book, then squeezed the book back into the shelves to apply pressure, but it is more effective to use a press, which distributes the pressure equally across the surface, and to change the paper, generally a combination of absorbent blotter paper and newspaper, often.

Flower presses are made in several designs, but the frequent changing of paper is more important than which style of press you use. One type of press is made of two smooth pieces of wood, about twelve inches by eight or nine inches. Through each of the four corners is a screw with a wing nut and bolt, and these are tightened down to apply the necessary pressure. Another design uses the smooth pieces of wood, but the turning of a center augur applies the pressure. A third design uses pieces of wood made into a latticework. Two leather or heavy cloth straps are wrapped around the two pieces of latticework and tightened with strap buckles to hold the press together and apply pressure. This third type is favored by botanical collectors as it is portable and lightweight. Heavy books or tiles can also be used to provide weight and distribution for pressing.

Naturally flat, relatively two-dimensional flowers and plants are the easiest to press—pansies and leaves, for example—while the multipetaled, deeply three-dimensional are more difficult—orchids, calla lilies, and peonies are examples of this latter type. Flowers and plants that have thick, fleshy stems, stamens, pistils, or other parts are difficult to press because they have so much moisture that they may not dry before decay starts. Professionals often use a scalpel to slice a thick stem or flower pistil in half, thus retaining the form and shape but reducing the mass of the slow-to-dry fleshy part. Flowers may be pressed face up or in a half or three-quarter profile, depending upon the type of flower and the desired result.

COLLECTING

〜〜

In the nineteenth century professional and amateur botanists alike roamed the globe searching for unusual plant specimens. Some collected the actual plants, either uprooting them or cutting specimens, most commonly drying them in portable presses. Others painted those plants they found, providing a record of their discoveries. Nature and things natural were in fashion, and pressed plants and plein-air painting were favored activities among people from all walks of life. While would-be artists trekked off into the country, set up their easels, and painted the glowing fields and hillsides, others packed up their plant presses and headed out to gather grasses, flowers, and leaves. At home, ladies—in particular ladies of leisure—gathered from their gardens and pressed such flowers as pansies or roses. The delicate results were used to adorn cards, notebooks, memory boxes, lamp shades and picture frames given as gifts or used to decorate their own parlors and boudoirs.

HARVESTING FOR PRESSING

Harvest when there is no visible moisture clinging to the plants, as excess moisture slows the drying process and invites mold and decay.

The moment of harvest depends upon which stage of development of the flowers, leaves, or grasses you want to preserve. The first small, soft-textured, apple green oak leaves picked in May when the tree has just begun to leaf out will be quite different from the large, leathery, dark green leaves picked in late summer. Violets in bud, partially open or fully open, will present different appearances but will press equally well.

PREPARING FOR PRESSING

To prepare for pressing, lay a sheet of absorbent paper, such as blotter paper, on the bottom of the press. Follow with several thicknesses of newspaper, then put the flowers or plants to be pressed on the newspaper or on another sheet of absorbent paper. Cover with more newspaper, then another sheet of absorbent paper. Several sets of layered plants may be made and numerous items pressed at the same time.

When pressing many layers it is best to insert additional sheets of wood or heavy cardboard between sets of plants to equalize the pressure. Put the layered sets into the press and apply pressure. The flowers should be held firmly but not crushingly tight. Keep the press in a warm, dry location, free from insects. If possible, change the newspaper twice a day and the absorbent paper daily. Check the progress of the drying until the flowers, leaves, or grasses are crisp but not brittle and the process is completed. Once dry, the flowers or plants may be stored in a box or other container, still between the sheets of newspaper and preferably flat, in a location safely away from moisture and insects.

Supplies

Entire shops are devoted to herbarium supplies. Here one can find a variety of different weights of acid-free mounting papers made from 100 percent cotton fiber, thick blotting papers, and acid-free manila folders. There will be thin linen tape and cotton thread for mounting and tying, scalpels, scissors, herbarium and annotation labels, and of course, professional presses.

Mounting

To mount a flower or other plant herbarium-style, start with a sheet of acid-free 100 percent cotton fiber paper to protect it from deteriorating and discoloring over time. There are two primary methods used: glue and ties.

For the gluing method a white glue, such as Elmer's, is commonly employed, although in the past protein-based glue made from rabbit or yak skin or the hooves of animals was used. On several thicknesses of newspaper, make a pool of glue large enough to cover the surface of the largest leaf or flower. Carefully lay the back of the flower or plant surface in the glue, then remove it from the glue, place it on the mounting paper, and gently affix it. Dot any stems with just enough glue to cover the stem and secure it on either side. Set the paper aside to dry.

To mount using the tying method, first arrange the subject on the paper, then with a needle, pierce a set of holes on either side of the stem through which to pass the cotton or linen thread. Pass it through the holes, and tie it in the back. Repeat as needed on multistemmed subjects.

Species tulips, unlike the modern hybrids, have diminutive flowers growing on stems that are commonly only six to twelve inches tall, the smallest being *Tulipa biflora*, which is a scant three inches. Species tulips are the wild tulips from which the modern hybrid tulips were first bred; their origins lie in the arid plateaus and rocky ravines of places such as Turkistan, Baluchistan, Turkey, and the Hindu Kush.

In the sixteenth century, the first tulips were introduced into Europe by a Flemish emissary of the Holy Roman emperor Ferdinand I who had been sent on a peace mission to Suleiman the Magnificent. On his way to the sultan's capital of Constantinople, he had seen flowers growing that were unknown in Europe. He purchased some bulbs of these flowers, and when he returned home, they were planted in Ferdinand's palace garden.

The fame of the tulips spread, and the Europeans, especially the Dutch, became so enamored of the delicate flowers that professionals and amateurs alike began to crossbreed them in a effort to create larger and more dramatic flowers in new colors and color combinations—the forerunners of today's hybridized modern tulips. The bulbs that produced these spectacular flowers became a high-priced commodity and sold for the modern equivalent of $3,000 to $30,000 each—founding the fortunes of horticultural empires and individuals alike. Tulip bulbs were purchased by adventurous members of the middle class who were gambling on a tulip's doubling (or more) its price in a month—which sometimes happened—allowing them to sell it for a tidy profit.

Tulip lust sent collectors and adventurers forth to Asia Minor, the arid Mediterranean islands, and Central Asia, where they ventured into far-off corners searching for hitherto unknown tulip varieties or species and new supplies of known ones for their breeding programs or for sale. Although the frenzy of tulip collecting, breeding, and trading—tulip mania, as it came to be called—had abated by the end of the century, the searching for, discovery, collecting, and classification by botanists of the wild species continued well into the twentieth century, as did also the rapacious collection of bulbs in the wild for sale in

Pressing Species Tulips

Harvest: When the flowers are half to fully open. Include stems and leaves if desired. *Tulipa batalinii* **is an exception, as its flowers do not fully open but stay in pointed bud forms. Note that colors of the petals may change from early to later stages of bloom.**

Preparation: If the stems are thick and fleshy, slice them in half before pressing.

Imagine pressed petals as a pattern adorning

light-filled windowpanes or shadowed

curtain veils. Pressed and lifted to the light, leaves

and petals take on a second life in forms

that bring new textures, colors, and patterns

into any room.

bulk to bulb purveyors. In 1990 the Dutch bulb industry, the world's largest, voluntarily entered into an agreement with several international environmental organizations to establish labeling laws in an effort to curtail the trade in wild bulbs, many of which are threatened species. They agreed that all Dutch exporters would begin labeling bulbs harvested from the wild "Bulbs from Wild Source"; that in 1992 cultivated minor bulb plants, which include species tulips, would be labeled "Bulbs Grown from Cultivated Stock"; and that in 1995 the cultivated major bulb varieties would also be so marked. Because of this thoughtful plan, it is most likely that any species tulip offered by a reputable Dutch supplier today will come from cultivated stock.

Of the dozens and dozens of species tulips, a number are readily available from specialty mail-order catalogue sources. They may be found listed as "botanical" tulips as well as wild and species tulips. Their colors range from brilliant red to subtle shades of bronze tinged with olive or rose, and the size of the plants varies from three to twelve inches tall. Leaves may be gray-green, bluish, or stippled with magenta. Their shapes too are varied: some thin and swordlike, others broad and curving, yet others ruffled at the edge and twisted and curled. Flowers resembling clustered creamy water lilies characterize *Tulipa turkestanica*, a plant only five inches tall. Deep red petals with a black blotch at the throat and curled, twisted leaves touched with wine red are the hallmarks of *T. wilsoniana*, a wild tulip from Central Asia that grows to six inches. Also from Central Asia are the *T. batalinii*, tiny specimens that grow five or six inches tall and bear blooms of either apricot orange, bright red, soft rosy yellow, orange-suffused yellow, or bronze on stubby, upright stems. All the species tulips lend themselves to pressing, but none is more dramatic than the orange-and-yellow spider-petaled *T. acuminata*, whose thin, twisting petals, four inches long, flatten into fascinating patterns.

Pressing Poppies

Harvest: When the flowers are one-third to three-quarters open, because fully opened flowers drop their petals quickly. Once the stem is cut, immediately sear the cut end with a flame and place it in water until ready to press. Pressing should be done as soon as possible.

Preparation: No special preparation required.

Poppies comprise a diverse group of flowers generally characterized by paper-thin, often translucent petals, which make them ideal candidates for easy pressing. One of the most unusual of the poppies is the Himalayan blue poppy, *Meconopsis betonicifolia*, throughout Europe a sought-after garden flower today, although it was not cultivated there until the early twentieth century when a professional British seed collector brought back seeds harvested from plants found growing along a river gorge in Tibet. Its silky petals of brilliant deep blue seem to reflect the intense blue of high mountain lakes and sky, making it most unusual in the panoply of poppies, and of flowers in general. The Iceland poppy, *Papaver nudicaule*, although considerably more common than the Himalayan blue poppy, is unusual in that the large, single-petaled parchmentlike flowers are bright yellow or orange, as well as white.

Most poppies are in the color range of red, pink, and white, like the wild red poppies that blanket the fields, meadows, and ravines of the Mediterranean countries from Spain to Israel in late spring and early summer. These are the Flanders Field poppies, *Papaver rhoeas*, also called corn

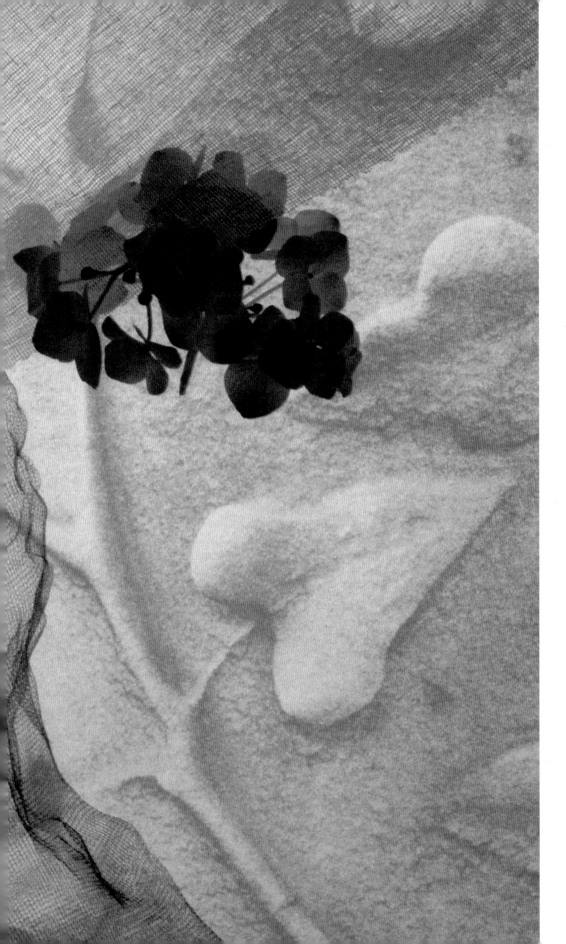

poppies, which became the symbol of the soldiers who died in World War I. Today, in front of post offices, banks, and city halls across the United States, Veterans of Foreign Wars sell red paper poppies atop stems of twisted green wire to commemorate the hundreds of thousands of soldiers who died on the battlefields of Europe between 1914 and 1918.

Impressionist painters captured the glow of the red poppies in the wheat fields, Claude Monet's paintings *Poppy Field* and *Path in the Île Saint-Martin, Vétheuil* being among the most notable. In fact, Monet was so fascinated with them that he gathered seeds from the wild and planted them in the flower gardens of his home at Giverny.

The oriental and somniferum poppies, glorious to look at in the garden in their rich hues of scarlet, salmon, white, and pink, have heavy, multipetaled heads that make them more difficult to press than the single-petaled types such as the Iceland, Flanders Field, California, and Himalayan poppies. The multipetaled types are more successfully dried flat on racks or in sand or silica gel.

Pressing Wild Grasses

Harvest: Green, before seed heads mature.

Preparation: No special preparation necessary.

Wild grasses grow no matter where one lives—even grasses that we often refer to as weeds, because we do not want them in our yards or gardens. Look not only to these wild grasses to dry, but also to the numerous varieties of ornamental grasses that are available either as part of a landscape or in a cutting garden. These can make beautiful pressed plants: pressing can capture the bend of the stems and the dip of the heads, animating the dried result with the spirit of the growing grass. Their subtle palette of earth tones, shades of green, brown, gold, and umber, make grasses less dramatic than brightly colored flowers, but their form more than compensates for their lack of bright color.

Grasses are best cut for pressing when young and before the head has filled with seed, particularly if it is a variety with a large seed head. Wheat, for example, has quite a large and heavy seed head, and it will not press flat. Alternatively, you can harvest grasses when the heads are formed but seeds not yet fully matured.

The pansy makes one of the finest of pressed decorative flowers because of its naturally flat flower face. Pansies as we know them today, with their rounded petals, ruffled, curving, or straight edges, blotched or lined centers, myriad color combinations, and varied size, are the result of hybridization and selection first done in England during the early part of the nineteenth century. The estate gardeners were among the most active and influential hybridizers of this period, and their employers encouraged them to pursue the creation and propagation of new varieties of flowers.

Wild pansies, or violas, had long been a familiar and popular feature of the English countryside, the dainty flowers called by names like Johnny-jump-up, love-in-idleness, and heartsease. The gardening craze of the nineteenth century extended to bringing in local plants from the wild to be cultivated in the garden. Hence the beginning of the selecting and crossbreeding of wild violas such as *Viola tricolor* and *V. lutea*, which had petals with lines radiating from the center. Crossbreeding and selecting created larger flowers and different color patterns. Out of this breeding appeared a

flower whose lines were fused together, making a blotch or the now-familiar pansy face. The new selections were then further crossed and selected to the extent that, as with roses and other extensively hybridized garden flowers, the parentage became obscured.

Pansies became enormously popular because they were a new bedding plant, and stylized outdoor flower beds were experiencing a vogue at the time. There was a great demand for more and more varieties and colors of the small flowering

Pressing Pansies

Harvest: Any time from bud stage to fully open.

Preparation: Remove stem if it seems fleshy, or slice the stem in half.

FLOWERS PRESSED IN PAPER, FONTAINE DE VAUCLUSE

~⤝⤞~

*For hundreds of years, the little mill at Fontaine de Vaucluse in the Luberon Mountains of Provence has been making paper impressed
with the wildflowers of the region—Cupid's dart, lavender, red poppies, and bracken. Here the Sorgue River erupts in a fountain from deep under-
ground, and the mill uses the river's energy to turn the paddles in its mixing vats, combining the pulp and wildflowers to make its special paper.*

plants used to create intricate patterns and borders in the landscape style popular during the late nineteenth century.

Pansies are still popular for beds, borders, window boxes, and container plantings of all kinds, particularly in Germany and Switzerland, where certain varieties are bred to bloom in fall and into winter, others specifically for spring and summer. Large-, medium-, and small-flowered types are available. One of the largest is 'Majestic Giant', which has flowers up to four inches in diameter in shades of yellow, violet, reddish orange, and lavender with medium to small dark blotches. Large-flowered, too, is the variety 'Imperial Antique Shades', whose unusual hues of rose, salmon, yellow, and cream combinations change colors as the flowers pass from bud to maturity. I especially like the wavy-petaled 'Super Chalon Giants', whose faces display lots of whiskery lines as well as large blotches on petals of rusty red, rose, crimson, violet, burgundy, and white. Other large-flowered pansies have blotches so large that only a small border of color surrounds the edges

of the petals. Although blotches are most frequently an inky color, increasingly we are seeing pansies with blotches of red, rose, and yellow. The pansy with perhaps the most unusual color—some might say unnatural—is 'Jolly Joker', which has a splash of bright orange on a deep purple petal.

Small-flowered pansies, violas, and sweet violets also exhibit interesting ranges of color combinations, blotches, and lines, but there are far fewer varieties of these commercially available than there are of the large-flowered pansies. Look for the old-fashioned Johnny-jump-up and for the small pure apricot pansies, butter yellow sweet violets, and 'Bowles Black' viola, which has deep indigo petals.

USING
SILVER SAND AND
SILICA GEL

Flowers dried with silver sand or silica gel look incredibly lifelike yet have an ethereal porcelain quality, retaining their original color and shape to a much greater extent than air-dried flowers. In this method the flowers are placed in a container face-up, face-down, or sideways, depending upon the type of flower, then surrounded and covered by the drying medium, whose fine grains hold and support each petal in a natural form as the flower dries. Silver sand, silica gel, borax, or a mixture of borax and cornmeal are all effective mediums for drying flowers. Silica gel is a granular dessicant made from silicon dioxide that absorbs moisture from the flower, speeding up the drying process. Sand, borax, and cornmeal are not true desiccants, and using them serves only to hold the flowers in position as they gradually dry.

An essential difference between using sand and using a desiccant is the timing factor. Flowers in silica gel must be checked frequently because if left too long in the desiccant, they will become brittle, shatter, and deteriorate, while flowers in sand or borax and cornmeal combinations are not

at risk. Generally speaking, flowers in silica will dry within several days to a week, those in borax and cornmeal combinations within two weeks, and those in sand only in about two weeks, but there remain numerous variables. Small flowers with light, papery petals will dry more quickly than heavy-headed, multipetaled flowers. Moisture content varies from flower to flower, and from one type of growing condition to another. Drying times will also vary according to climate and season. The best insurance for success is to experiment to determine the time needed for drying specific flowers under your particular conditions.

Silver sand, which was commonly used for drying flowers in the nineteenth century and earlier, was, in spite of its glamorous name, simply clean, fine sand from riverbeds or beaches from which all traces of silt or other elements had been removed by sifting and rinsing it enough times to render it pristine. Any good quality common sand can be used for drying, but the finer the sand and the cleaner, the less likely it is to damage the flower petals. Coarse sand has sharp edges that nick and pock the petals, as does debris such as bits of broken stems, splinters, or shells.

Although out of fashion today, superseded by the quicker-acting silica gel, sand has several virtues to recommend it. There is virtually no danger of overdrying and thus shattering brittle petals, nor does it leave behind traces of powder on the flowers as do silica gel and borax or borax mixtures. Sand is also particularly useful for drying flowers that have multiple layers of cupped petals, as the miniscule grains of sand can be sifted into the thicket of petals to ensure that every bit of the flower is in contact with them, which is more difficult to do with the larger-grained silica.

Borax and cornmeal are often used together in combinations varying from half and half to two parts borax to one part cornmeal. The varying proportions have more to do with availability and personal preference than with drying effectiveness.

HARVESTING FOR DRYING WITH SAND, SILICA GEL, BORAX, OR CORNMEAL

Harvesting may be done at any time when the flowers are between one-quarter to fully open and no moisture is visible. Buds may be harvested as well, but large, thick buds may be difficult to dry successfully. Leaves and stems may be left attached, or removed.

Although sand, silica gel, borax, and cornmeal all have different properties, the method for using them to dry flowers is nearly the same. The most important difference is that silica requires an airtight container such as a tin to prevent it from absorbing moisture from the air, and the others require open containers to allow for maximum air circulation to aid in drying.

Most flowers are dried face up, with or without the stem. Some schools of thought recommend removing the stems and replacing them with wires before drying; others suggest removing the stems, drying them separately, and wiring the flower head to be dried with a short piece that can be used later to reattach the original or another stem; finally, there are advocates of leaving the stem attached. The choice seems to be a matter of personal style, the intended use of the dried flowers, and the size of the containers being used.

For face-up drying in sand, fill the container with enough sand or other medium to allow the stem to be placed upright yet with enough headroom in the container to cover the flower with the sand. If you are drying more than one flower, make sure the petals are not touching. Because sand flows so readily, a good way to get it into the deepest curls and crevices of the flower is to build a "wall" of sand about the flower, letting the sand flow from your hand. Then gently tip the container, letting the sand flow across and through the petals and find its own level. Continue until only the top of the flower is exposed, then dribble sand through your hand across it. Finish by covering the flower with at least an inch of sand. Alternatively, scoop out a hole in the

POPULAR VICTORIAN PASTIMES

≈⌇≈

Drying flowers and leaves in silver sand was a popular pastime with Victorian ladies, and magazines and books of the period advised their readers on technique, on choice of flowers, and on how to use the dried flowers for decoration. At a museum in London, there is a place card on display in a glass case. The card, with someone's name still faintly legible, was presumably from a long-ago dinner party and is decorated with a dried pansy. The identifying label in the case says simply, "Place card with pansy dried in silver sand."

sand large enough to hold the flower, place the flower in the hole, and drizzle in sand to fill the hole and cover the flower, gently shifting the container from side to side to allow the sand to flow. Do not shift once the top of the flower is covered. Continue covering until there is at least a one-inch layer of sand over the top of the flower.

For horizontal positioning in sand, scoop out a hole and lay the flower into it. Drizzle the sand and shift the container as described above. For drying face down, make a small mound of sand in the bottom of the container, place the flower face down on top of it, and drizzle sand around the flower until there is at least a one-inch layer of sand covering it. Use borax and cornmeal mixtures the same as you would sand. Sometimes a little extra assist from a small paintbrush or spoon is needed to get the borax or cornmeal deep into the heart of the flower as these do not flow as easily as sand.

Once the flowers are covered with the sand or borax and cornmeal, place the container in a warm, dry location. Check the flowers for dryness every few days by gently brushing or pushing aside the drying medium until a few petals are exposed. Once they feel papery to the touch, expose the flowers one at a time by tipping the container and carefully pouring off the drying medium while one hand supports the dried flower until it is freed. Flowers dried using borax and cornmeal will need to be dusted off with a paintbrush or soft cotton as the drying medium, unlike sand, leaves them covered with a film of powder.

To store the flowers, carefully wrap them in paper and put them into a box. Keep the box in a dry location. Alternatively, leave the dried flowers on the surface of the sand or borax and cornmeal mixture with the stems pushed down, and keep them in a dry, dark place.

Dry flowers in silica gel the same way as in borax and cornmeal, but use an airtight container. Check daily for dryness. Once the flowers are dry, dust away any bits of powder and store the flowers loosely covered in a dry location. Some floral

designers use hair spray or another fixative to form a barrier against moisture on their dried flowers, particularly those dried with silica gel, as they tend to reabsorb moisture and wilt if placed in a humid situation.

Miniature roses are quite successful dried in sand or silica gel. Because they are so small, their unusual coloration and unique and delicate forms are lost in the inevitable shrinkage that occurs during the air-drying process. Miniature roses, defined as small rosebushes with small leaves and flowers in proportion to the size of the plant, have become exceedingly popular in the last twenty-five years, particularly in the United States, and extensive efforts have gone into breeding the hundreds of different varieties of these flowers. Plants are generally between twelve and eighteen inches tall, and some are climbers. Those plants that are larger than miniature rosebushes but smaller than a full-size bush are likely to be classified as patio roses or ground cover roses.

Drying Miniature Roses in Sand

Harvest: Anytime from bud to fully open, with stems approximately three inches long or clipped to one-quarter inch.

Position: Place stem-end down, bloom face up. Buds may also be placed horizontally.

The modern introduction of the miniature rose appears to have begun with a bright pink rose growing in a pot on a windowsill in Switzerland. It was owned by a Colonel Roulet, a friend of Henri Correvan, who was a breeder of roses; the colonel gave Correvan a cutting from which Correvan propagated the miniature roses that he introduced to the market in 1920, naming the rose after his friend, 'Rouletii'. During the next decade a young Californian, Ralph Moore, began breeding these roses, working initially with 'Rouletii'. From that start in the 1930s, he has bred hundreds of varieties of miniatures, including a number of moss roses. In 1948 he began trying to produce an ever-blooming miniature moss rose, and fifteen years later he introduced 'Fairy Moss', the first. Today, Ralph Moore is universally acknowledged as having had a major influence on the breeding and popularizing of miniature roses worldwide.

Their small size and repeated and extended blooming period, along with the myriad nuances of colors they exhibit, have made these roses increasingly appreciated for their intrinsic value, not just as a passing trend. As tiny replicas of larger roses, the miniatures display not only the characteristic high, pointed bud shapes of the modern roses, but also the cupped, quartered, and reflexed petal characteristics of the old roses. The flowers may be multi-petaled or single-petaled, the bushes thorny or thornless, the blooms in candelabra clusters and sprays or atop single stems. Some, like 'Daniela' and 'Renny', have pointed petals that resemble those of water lilies; others have softly rounded petals with tips that curl back like those of 'Rainbow's End'. 'Dresden Doll', a tiny moss rose, has petals that form a perfect cup. 'Oriental Simplex' is a single-petal rose with five brilliant scarlet petals, the bases of which are tipped with gold and surround a cluster of long, golden stamens. 'Pinstripe' and 'Stars 'n Stripes' are variegated shades of white, red, and pink, while 'Pandemonium', another of the many variegated roses, is bright red-and-yellow. In short, the miniatures encompass nearly all the possibilities available in full-size roses.

Narcissus of all types have soft, papery petals that when dried in sand or silica gel retain the airy, near-translucent quality that makes them such a beloved part of the spring garden landscape. Narcissus, a group of flowering bulbs that belong to the amaryllis family and include daffodils and jonquils, are quite varied in size, shape, and color, and many of them are notable for their intense fragrance.

Those with cups longer than their petals are generally referred to as daffodils or trumpet daffodils. 'King Alfred', a sturdy yellow one introduced in 1899, remains one of the most popular of daffodils today, though the numerous new pink-trumpeted or bicolored types are more flamboyant.

Drying Narcissus in Silica Gel

Harvest: When one-quarter to fully opened.

Position: Place stem upright or at a slight angle, with bloom as nearly natural as possible.

The pink of the trumpets may be a salmon hue, or apricot, coral, or rose and may be pastel or intensely colored. 'Royal Scarlet' has a reddish orange trumpet and large, deep yellow petals. 'General Patton' has a frilly yellow trumpet but bright white petals.

Large- and small-cupped narcissus form another category. Their cups are shorter than the trumpet cups of the daffodils. Literally dozens and dozens of different varieties are available within this category, and it is quite a fruitful one to search for flowers of unusual color combinations and shapes. 'Barrett Browning' has cups of saffron orange and creamy ivory petals and 'Ambergate', one of my particular favorites, has amber petals surrounding a large cup brilliantly colored in carnelian red. 'Petit Four' not only has a frilly double cup, but the cup itself is a lush apricot pink surrounded by large white petals.

There are also narcissus with ruffled doubled centers or reflexing petals, some that bloom in dangling clusters, some with upright clusters, and some in miniature size. The 'Pheasant's Eye' is one of the oldest of the narcissus, probably cultivated since ancient times, and is said to have a fragrance so intense and sweet that a dozen blooms will overwhelm an ordinary-sized room. Of equal fragrance is the narcissus 'Chinese Sacred Lily', whose spiced nutmeg and mace scent wafts on the air to create fragrance-laden pools. Both these narcissus have small orange cups and ivory petals, but however nice it would be, the fragrance does not linger once the flowers have been dried, so enjoy their heady scent before burying the flowers in sand or silica to dry.

As the flowers of the narcissus group mature, the seed head, which is located at the base of the bloom, becomes larger, fleshier, and more pronounced. It is best to harvest narcissus for drying as soon as they have opened, as the more developed the seed head, the longer the flower will have to be left to dry. Drying long enough to ensure

Pillows, lamp shades, clothing, picture frames—

silica-dried blossoms give everyday objects

a fresh personality. Forest moss pulled from fallen

trees or daffodils saved from a spring rain

can be gathered, dried, and applied to create

indoor magic.

that the fleshy part as well as the petals are dried creates the risk that the petals will become overdried and brittle. Positioning of narcissus in the desiccant is important, because in nature the blooms tend to face downward or outward, and to place them strictly stem-down, head-up is to force them into an unnatural position. Moreover, you may inadvertently snap the head while trying to do it, especially if working with one of the larger-headed types. Of course, you can always dry the blooms without the stem, but if you wish to keep the stems, place them at a slight angle in the desiccant, and carefully fill in around the heads with the desiccant to avoid a dried flower that is flat on one side and splayed on the other.

Zinnias have an exuberant range of colors, from primary red and yellow to delicate shades of mauve, dusty rose, lavender, cream and on to bright pink, carmine, and orange, all of which remain true, just slightly darker, when dried in sand or silica gel. Like the narcissus, the zinnia has paper-thin petals and hollow stems and dries quite quickly, and the flower head,

though often large, is not fleshy and spongy. However, many of the zinnia varieties have dense, multilayered petals—'Beehive' and 'Lilliput', for example—and it is difficult to ensure that even very fine sand can reach all the way to the petal base. Less tightly petaled and therefore easier to preserve are the 'Giant Cactus' zinnias with pointed petals and the round-petaled 'Giant Double' variety. In both types, the petals are attached to a flower head that increases in size as the flowers mature, opening up space between the petals.

Zinnias and dahlias, native to Mexico, are both members of the Compositae family. The family name derives from the flower heads, which are a composite of many small flowers or florets. If you look carefully at the center of a zinnia flower head, for example, you will see a collection of tiny yellow florets. Among the quickest and easiest of all summer flowers to grow, zinnias need only mediocre ground, water, and sun—the same requirements as the other simple-to-grow members of the Compositae family, sunflowers, cosmos, and bachelor's buttons. Their large seeds are easily handled, germinate within a week when planted in warm soil, and produce flowering plants sixty days

later, making them a good choice for an easy-to-grow cutting garden and an abundant source of flowers for drying.

Dahlias, like zinnias, dry exceptionally well in silica gel. Because they have continued to be extensively hybridized since the early nineteenth century dahlia craze, one can choose from hundreds of variations on shapes and colors. Dahlias raised from seed sent from the New World were growing in the botanical gardens in Madrid, Spain, for over a hundred years before they were rediscovered by the northern Europeans, setting off the dahlia craze. The continued appeal of dahlias as both landscaping and cutting flowers then and now is their wide range of colors, from soft pastels to brilliant oranges, combined with their ability to bloom over an extended period of time, providing reliable color from early summer into fall.

The species dahlias from which the modern ones were developed were bright red and single-petaled, but by 1809 a dark red, double-petaled type had been developed, and by 1840 there were dozens of different double- and single-petaled types in many colors, including a popular bright yellow.

Dahlias are technically grouped into sixteen different categories according to their flower shape and structure; each category has the entire span of colors, as well as various flower sizes and plant heights. We usually think of dahlias as being grown from tubers, but they are readily grown from seed as well, although the flowers will be more variable, which I find quite exciting. As the plants grow and bloom, the opening of each flower has an element of surprise, and at the end of the season the tubers of the most appealing flowers can be dug and stored for planting the following spring.

Peonies are among the most spectacular of flowers dried in silica gel or sand because their color and shape are so clearly preserved. Air-dried their petals wrinkle and crumple like crepe paper, which, although a nice effect, is quite different from that achieved with silica or sand. Silica gel preserves the sleek texture of a peony's petals, whether the original flower was a fluffy sphere or a row of single petals curving around long golden stamens.

Among the early breeders and popularizers of peonies were the nurserymen in England. In 1874 one nursery alone offered for sale over 850 different varieties, many of them scented. The introduction of *Paeonia lactiflora (albiflora)*, a fragrant peony whose origins are in the regions of Tibet, China, and Siberia, allowed hybridizers to create peonies with a rich, delicate fragrance similar to that of roses. This new attribute, plus a greater and greater size and variety of form and coloring, increased interest in peonies both in England and abroad.

Drying Zinnias and Dahlias in Silica Gel

Harvest: When the flowers are three-quarters to nearly fully open. Once dried, petals may drop from overmature flower heads.

Position: Stem down, head facing upward.

Sand drying invites intimate views of the singular

beauty found in elegant garden roses or rustic

sunflowers. The natural grace of a garland or a

simple bowl of dried objects can turn an empty

tabletop or wall into a creative stage.

Huge specimens were shown at the popular flower and garden shows of the late nineteenth and early twentieth centuries, where peonies, considered exotic, were quite a popular exhibitor's plant. Amateur and professional breeders and horticulturalists alike competed, showing off the achievements of their gardens.

Most of today's available garden or herbaceous peonies are derived in some way from *P. lactiflora hybrids*, but there has been such extensive breeding over the last hundred years that the newer varieties may not be fragrant. Peony trees, by contrast, are hybrids not from *P. lactiflora* but from another species, *P. suffruticosa*, and may or may not have a fragrance. Peony trees are capable of producing enormous blooms with heads so heavy they bend their branches with their weight, and these, successfully dried, are truly a stunning sight.

Peonies are well suited to drying in silica gel or in sand, but doing so requires patience, especially with the fluffy double types, to ensure that the granules or grains of the drying medium reach to the tightly packed base of the flower head.

Drying Peonies in Silica Gel

Harvest: When three-quarters to fully open and no moisture is visible.

Position: Place stem down, face up.

WAXING, SUGARING, OVEN-DRYING, AND FREEZE-DRYING

Waxing, sugaring, oven-drying, and freeze-drying are all methods of preserving flowers. Waxing and sugaring coat the flowers, leaves, or fruits with a covering that seals them from moisture. Oven-drying in a slow oven removes the moisture from them, as does freeze-drying.

Wax may be applied to fresh flowers and leaves of all kinds, and some fruits as well. A much more widely practiced technique during the nineteenth and early twentieth centuries than it is today, waxing provided flowers and leaves for still-life arrangements for tabletops and mantels in homes across Europe and North America. Generally the arrangements were protected from dust and insects by glass bells or cloches that were placed over them, and away from heat and direct sunlight, the waxed flowers would keep for years. Waxed flowers continued to be used until the 1950s, when an extensive variety of readily available air-dried flowers, many of them imported from Europe and Asia, supplanted waxed flowers in popularity.

WAXING FLOWERS

The process for waxing flowers is quite simple. Holding the short stems with tongs, or if a long stem, with your fingers, dip a fresh, unblemished flower or leaf in a pan of melted paraffin, and gently turn and dip the flower until it is fully coated with wax. Remove it from the wax and hold it over the pan for a minute or two to catch the drips. To let the wax harden around the flower and stem completely, hang the flower head down, attaching it by its stem to a stretched cord or wire in a location out of the sun and away from a heat source. Place several sheets of newspaper beneath the hanging flowers to catch any further drips. They may also be laid flat on trays, covered with wax paper or aluminum foil, and left there to harden.

Once the wax has hardened, remove the flower from the cord or wire or peel back the wax paper or foil, and using a sharp knife, carefully trim away any excess bits of wax. Repeat the dripping and hardening process several times to achieve the desired thickness. Wrap the waxed flowers in tissue paper and store in a cool place away from the light until ready to use them.

MAGNOLIA LEAVES AND WAXED FLOWERS

⤙⤚

In the early part of this century, memorial wreaths were made of preserved magnolia leaves dyed very dark and then decorated with waxed flowers. The preserving of the leaves was done in three different locations—Evergreen, Alabama; Besen, Illinois; and San Francisco, California— by five different companies. Three of the companies were headed by men of Danish origin, two by men of German origin, all using a preserving technique developed by I. G. Farben, a German chemical company. First the leaves were dyed in big vats full of hot dyes in colors of red, brown, or green. From there they were scooped out and put into a chemical solution that fixed the color and kept the leaves supple. Finally they were scooped out again and put into wooden crates, which were then racked, slightly tilted, to allow the leaves to drain and dry. The best leaves, those that were adequately dry and as supple as fine leather, were packed and shipped to florists from coast to coast, where they were made into wreaths that were decorated with wax flowers and red, white, and blue ribbons.

Preparing the Paraffin for
Waxing Flowers

Paraffin may be purchased at hardware
stores and generally comes in packages that
contain four blocks. To melt enough paraffin to dip and coat six to eight medium-
sized flowers, put two blocks of paraffin in
a heat-proof container, such as a coffee can,
reserved for this purpose. Because paraffin
is quite flammable, do not put the container
over direct heat. Instead, place it in a pan of
simmering water. As the paraffin melts, stir
it. When it has liquefied, it is ready to use.

SUGARING FLOWERS

Sugaring flowers and fruits is easily done
with egg whites, a paintbrush, and
superfine sugar, and this was a very popular
method of presenting fruits at Victorian
teas and dinner parties. Sometimes the
fruits to be sugared had been previously
steeped in sweetened brandy, and biting
through their sugared crust to the sweet-
fire taste of the fruit beneath was a well-
appreciated pleasure. Tiny edible flowers
such as violets or rose petals and small
leaves such as those of mint were sugared

Flower blossoms and tiny fruit become the
perfect foil for sugaring to preserve their beauty.
A child's party, an engagement, or a tea are
occasions for bringing these ethereal offerings into
everyday life. These edible charms delight the
senses with their sweet presentation.

too, and these either were served as candies for nibbling or used to garnish cakes and other sweets.

The less convoluted, ribbed, or heavily petaled the flower to be sugared and the more three-dimensional it or the fruit, the greater the success of the finished product, especially for amateurs. Once sugared, the flowers or fruits will need to be thoroughly dried before storing and then kept away from any humidity.

Choosing Edible Flowers

Although roses, pansies, nasturtiums, violets, and the blossoms of culinary herbs such as basil, borage, thyme, and cilantro are perhaps the most well known of edible flowers, they are also among the most palatable. Though many flowers are edible, they may be unpleasantly bitter or astringent. Here are some that have pleasant flavors and would be good choices for sugaring:

Calendula

Citrus blossoms

English daisy

Rose geranium

Hibiscus

Honeysuckle

Lavender

Lilac

Sugaring Rose Petals and Mint Leaves

For twelve rose petals and twelve mint leaves, you will need three egg whites and one cup of superfine sugar. Place the egg whites in a bowl and, using a fork or whisk, beat them until frothy but not stiff. Lay the petals and leaves on a piece of waxed paper and put the sugar in a bowl.

Using a small paintbrush, paint a petal or leaf on both sides with the egg whites, then put it into the bowl and spoon sugar over it. Using tweezers, carefully lift it up and shake off excess sugar. Return to the waxed paper to dry.

Repeat. If the egg whites lose their frothiness, beat them again. Let the petals and leaves stand overnight in a dry location. Once dry, put them in a tin, a glass jar, or a paper bag and store it in a cool, dry place.

* Remember, use only unsprayed, pesticide-free flowers that you know are edible.

OVEN-DRYING

Flowers, leaves, and some thinly sliced fruits may be dried in an oven set between 175 and 200 degrees Fahrenheit. Single petals and leaves of all kinds are most suitable for this treatment as they dry more quickly than heavy-petaled full flower heads, whose outer edges are prone to crisping before the heavier center is fully dried. For the larger heads, consider starting the process in the oven and finishing by air-drying on racks.

A truly sumptuous potpourri of colors, shapes, and scents can quickly be accomplished by oven-drying. I gather the petals from my parrot tulips as they fall, either in the garden or from their vase inside. I spread the petals on a baking sheet and put them in a slow, slow oven just long enough to dry them, about twenty minutes. Once they are dry, I store the petals in a paper bag or tin until I am ready to use them.

I follow the same process with my roses, but I use primarily the petals from the ultrafragrant old roses such as the bright pink *Rosa rugosa* 'Rubra', purple-hued hybrid perpetual 'Reine de Violettes',

Oven-Drying Sage Leaves

Set an oven to 175 degrees Fahrenheit. Spread the sage leaves on a baking sheet. Put the baking sheet in the oven and bake for approximately thirty minutes, checking the leaves after ten minutes to make sure they are not burning. After fifteen minutes, toss the leaves. The leaves are done when they feel papery to the touch but not brittle.

Remove the leaves from the oven and let them cool. Then, put them in a tin, glass jar, or paper bag and store them in a cool, dry place, where they will keep for six months or longer.

Water in its solid state becomes a showcase for the

brilliant flowers of summer. Creating a

flower-filled ice bucket momentarily suspends

nature's beauty from a frozen beginning to

a disappearance by evening's end to celebrate the

fleeting beauty of nature.

and the magenta moss rose 'William Lobb'. Other fragrant choices for oven-drying are sage leaves, lemon verbena, and mint.

FREEZE-DRYING

Numerous types of flowers, fruits, and vegetables can be freeze-dried, rendering the original virtually unchanged other than becoming more intense in color and reduced in weight. A large, freeze-dried, dinner-plate dahlia, its brilliant purple-and-white petals looking lush and succulent, has no more weight in the hand than a dandelion puff.

In other methods of drying flowers, the water in the flowers is a liquid when it is removed from the cells of the plant, and the cell walls are ruptured during removal. The change in appearance between the fresh and the dried is caused by the collapse of the cell walls and the consequent loss of pigment. In freeze-drying, however, the cell walls stay relatively intact because the water is removed as a vapor, which can pass through the cell walls without damaging them.

Freeze-drying, unlike other methods of flower drying or preserving, requires a serious investment in a specialized piece of equipment—a freeze-dryer. Freeze-dryers have two airtight cylindrical chambers, one large, one small. The flowers are placed on racks in the larger chamber (a medium-sized machine may hold up to three thousand blossoms), the cylinders sealed, and the temperature set to -20 degrees Fahrenheit in the larger product chamber and to -70 degrees Fahrenheit in the smaller chamber, the ice bank. The machine's vacuum pump then begins to remove the air from the chambers, because, in an atmosphere with greatly reduced pressure, water in a solid state—the ice in the flowers—will change to a vapor without becoming a liquid. Consequently, the moisture in the flowers moves as a vapor into the surrounding atmosphere, where it is drawn to the other much colder chamber and frozen again into a solid, becoming a block of ice. Successive blocks are removed until there is no longer any discernible moisture present, then the machine is shut off and the flowers removed. The length of time needed to accomplish this process

varies from several days to several weeks, depending upon what is being dried. Vegetables such as artichokes, cauliflower, and eggplants take considerably more time than begonias.

Because freeze-dried flowers will reabsorb moisture, they must undergo a treatment to seal them and protect them. Different types of sprays and dips that do this are available, and some have an ultraviolet inhibiting agent to preserve the color of the bloom as well as seal its surface.

Freeze-dried flowers look so fresh and touchable that from a distance it is almost impossible to tell that they are not fresh. They are preserved in such a lifelike, unblemished fashion that they seem imperishable, a fact that accounts for their increasing popularity, turning a page toward the future of *les immortelles*.

Acknowledgments

So many, many generous people shared their time, knowledge, and creativity to make this book possible—we thank you all.

Michaele Thunen, artist, stylist, organizer, and resourcer *par excellence* is an extraordinary colleague and was a pleasure and inspiration to work with; as always; Jackie Jones, Kristen Jester, and Katie Nash of Jacqueline Jones Design bent their creative and imaginative wills to the task of making the design of the book soar.

Dr. Allan Armitage of University of Georgia at Athens who shared his knowledge and enthusiasm for all aspects of flowers, fresh and dried; Sally Ferguson of the Bulb Research Center in Brooklyn, New York, who provided the most current information on the trade in wild bulbs; Knut Nielson Jr. of Evergreen, Alabama, for sharing his family story of three-quarters of a century in the flower trade; Van Oium at Northstar Freeze-dry Manufacturing in Minnesota for his technical information on freeze-drying; Kieft Seeds in Holland for arranging visits to large and small commercial dried flower producers; Charlotte Glenn, generous as always with her botanical and horticultural expertise and equipment; Dr. Bruce Bartholomew and Janet Jones of the Academy of Sciences, San Francisco, California, who so kindly took time to show us the Acadamy's herbaria and allowed us to photograph there; Augustin Thieffery of Vilmorin Seeds in France for first showing me the original Vilmorin-Andrieux aquarelles; David Jefferey of Unwins Seeds in Cambridge, England, who has shared his passion and knowledge of English horticulture and its history with me

over the years; to our editors at Chronicle Books, Leslie Jonath and Bill LeBlond, and to Michael Carabetta, Pamela Geismar and Gretchen Scoble whose confidence in our vision of this book never wavered and who were a staunch support to us throughout; Virginia Rich who so carefully and thoughtfully copyedited the manuscript; Susan Lescher, a superb agent who is always there when needed; Jim Schrupp, who never flinched at speaking the truth and cheering the grey days; Ethel Brennan and Oliver Brennan, Tom and Dan Schrupp, children who understand; and a special thank you to Michael Schwab, Eric and Peter, Kathryn's greatest fans; and to Ed Haverty, Michaele's steadfast and enthusiastic partner.

So many artists contributed their creative works to make this book special: Pouke', Chloe Halpern, David Turner and John Martin of Turner and Martin; Alice Erb and Lauren Allard of Tail of the Yak; Ron Morgan of Ron Morgan Floral Designs; Vicki Prosek, Gail Peachen, Toni Elling of Meadowsweets; Joseph Schmidt of Joseph M. Schmidt Chocolates; Mike and Debbie Schramer of Whimsical Twigs; Marcia Atkinson of Gardenhouse; and Claudia Schwartz and Toby Hansen of Bell'occhio.

The flowers that made this book possible came from many, many generous flower lovers. Ray Giacopazzi of Hillcrest Gardens, flower grower *extraordinaire*, contributed dozens of wondrous freeze-dried flowers and fruits of all kinds; Suzie Eglin of Kisetsu custom dried in silica all kinds of flowers and was always ready to experiment, as well as loaning us props;

Barbara Atkinson and Karen Baba of Plan Decor let us use some of their most unusual freeze-dried flowers and fruits; from Sean Quigley and Peter Kline of Paxton Gate came a collection of unusual pods, calyxes, and other natural materials; Ron and Pam Kaiser of Westside Farms, Linda Hauser of Sunflower, Rosie Echelmeier of Marin Country Floral Art, and the staff at Coast Wholesale all donated special materials for us to use; Paul Herbertz gave us dahlias and begonias to dry; Howard Garrison of the USDA germplasm repository who gave us a dozen different varieties of their gorgeous figs to dry.

Kind people allowed us to photograph in their beautiful California homes: Barbara, Spencer, and Lindsey Hoopes, San Francisco; Carla, David, and J. D. Nasaw, Ross, California; Stephen Brady, San Francisco; and Jenn Kissler who facilitated; Candace Barnes, San Francisco; Jan Dutton, Ross, California; Lauren, Paul, Sennet, and Haven Allard, Oakland, and also Tail of the Yak, Berkeley.

Production and photography assistants who were at hand throughout: Terry Greene, Cachet Bean, Helga Sigvaldadóttir, and Rachel Weill. And for their extra support and props: Margareta Lindé, Delmy Rivera, Susan and Hans Nehme, and Betty Jane Roth.

Bibliography

Armitage, Allan M. *Specialty Cut Flowers*.
    Portland: Varsity Press/Timber Press,
    1993.

Austin, David. *Shrub Roses and Climbing Roses*.
    Woodbridge, UK: Antique Collectors'
    Club Ltd., 1993.

Bullivant, Elizabeth. *Dried Fresh Flowers
    From Your Garden*. London: Pelham
    Books/Stephen Greene Press, 1989.

Clayton-Payne, Andrew. *Flower Gardens of
    Victorian England*. New York: Rizzoli,
    1988.

"Commercial Field Production of Cut and
    Dried Flowers". A National Symposium
    sponsored by The Center for Alternative
    Crops and Products, University of
    Minnesota and The American Society of
    Horticultural Science. December 6–8,
    1988.

Davies, Jennifer. *The Victorian Flower Garden*.
    London: BBC Books, 1991.

—*The Victorian Kitchen Garden*. London:
    BBC Books, 1987.

Elliott, Charles. "Tibet's Great Blue Poppy."
    Horticulture, Vol. LXXII, No. 5, May
    1994.

Hortus Third Dictionary. New York:
    Macmillan, 1976.

Lawrence, George H. M., editor. *America's
    Garden Legacy: A Taste for Pleasure*.
    Philadelphia: The Pennsylvania
    Horticultural Society, 1978.

McCann, Sean. *Miniature Roses, Their Care
    and Cultivation*. Harrisburg: Stackpole
    Books, 1991.

Frederick McGourty, editor. *Dried Flower
    Designs. Brooklyn Botanic Garden Record*,
    Vol. 30, No. 3 , #76.
    New York: Botanic Gardens, Inc., 1974.

Meunier, Christiane. *Lavandes et Lavandins*.
    Aix-en-Provence: Edisud, 1985.

Middleton, Dorothy. *Victorian Lady Travellers*.
    New York: Dutton,1965. Reprinted with
    new introduction. Chicago: Academy
    Chicago Publishers, 1982.

Moore, Ralph S. *The Breeding and Development
    of Modern Moss Roses*. Visalia: Moore-
    Sequoia, 1978.

Phillips, Roger and Martyn Rix. *The Random
    House Guide to Roses*. New York: Random
    House, 1988.

Proceedings of the 4th National Conference on
    Specialty Cut Flowers. Association of
    Specialty Cut Flower Growers, Inc.
    Cleveland, Ohio, November 1–4, 1991.

Robinson, William. *The English Flower Garden*.
    15th edition. London: J. Murray, 1933.
    U.K. reprint. A Ngaere Macray Book,
    NewYork: The Amaryllis Press, 1984.

"Waxing Lyrical". *Gardens Illustrated*.. Issue 10,
    October/November 1994.

Vilmorin-Andrieux et Cie. 1894. *Les Fleurs de
    Pleine Terre*. 1989 reprint, Les Editions
    1900.

Resources

Tail of the Yak – Berkeley, CA.

Gardenhouse – Burlingame, CA

Bell'occhio – San Francisco, CA

Turner and Martin – Palo Alto, CA

ABH Designs – New York, NY

Ron Morgan Floral Designs – Oakland, CA

Meadowsweets – Middleburgh, NY

Joseph M. Schmidt Chocolates –
    San Francisco, CA

Katrina Roselle Patisserie –
    Alamo and Berkeley, CA

David M. Bryan – Walnut Creek, CA

Whimsical Twigs – Ocean Park, WA

Marin Country Floral Art –
    San Anselmo, CA

Hillcrest Gardens – Petaluma, CA

Kisetsu – San Anselmo, CA

Plan Decor – Burlingame, CA

Paxton Gate – San Francisco, CA

Coast Wholesale – San Francisco, CA

Westside Farms – Healdsburg, CA

Herbarium Supply Company –
    Menlo Park, CA

Index

Georgeanne Brennan is a garden and food writer who divides her time between her small farm in Northern California and her home in Provence. Her features appear regularly in the *San Francisco Chronicle*, and she contributes to numerous publications, including *Bon Appétit*, *Metropolitan Home*, and *Garden Design*. She is also the author of *Potager: Fresh Garden Cooking in the French Style*; *The Glass Pantry: Preserving Seasonal Flavors*; and several books in the Garden Style series, including *Fragrant Flowers* and *Easy Roses*, all published by Chronicle Books.

Kathryn Kleinman, winner of a 1993 James Beard award for photography, specializes in food and flower images. Her work has appeared extensively in national advertising campaigns and magazines such as *Victoria* and *Garden Design*. Her groundbreaking volumes *Salad*, *Sushi*, *On Flowers*, and *The Glass Pantry*, all published by Chronicle Books, have brought her international recognition. She lives and works in Marin County, California.

Acclaimed San Francisco–based designer Jacqueline Jones has worked on books and other award-winning projects for corporate, university, and nonprofit clients since 1979. Other Chronicle books featuring her unique design style include *Salad*, *Openers*, *Fruit*, and *The Glass Pantry*.

Michaele Thunen is a floral and prop stylist who specializes in natural materials. She has produced and art directed in collaboration with photographers and advertising clients on such projects as *On Flowers* and *The Glass Pantry*. She lives in Berkeley, California.